CARL SAGAN
In Contact with the Cosmos

Great Scientists

CARL SAGAN
In Contact with the Cosmos

Jeremy Byman

MORGAN REYNOLDS Incorporated
Greensboro

CARL SAGAN: IN CONTACT WITH THE COSMOS

Morgan Reynolds, Inc., 620 S. Elm St., Suite 384
Greensboro, North Carolina 27406 USA

Picture credits: Unless otherwise noted, photographs are courtesy of the Library of Congress.

Library of Congress-Cataloging-in-Publication Data

Byman, Jeremy, 1944-
Carl Sagan : in contact with the cosmos / Jeremy Byman
p. cm. -- (Great scientists)
Includes bibliographical references and index.
Summary: A biography of the scientist who brought his passion for astronomy to the public through his television appearances on the "Tonight Show," his television series "Cosmos," and the feature film "Contact."
ISBN 1-883846-55-2 (lib. bdg.)
1. Sagan, Carl, 1934---Juvenile literature. 2. Astronomers--United States--Biography--Juvenile literature. [1. Sagan, Carl, 1934- 2.Astronomers.] I. Title. II. Great scientists (Greensboro, N.C.)

QB36.S15 .B96 2000
520'.92--dc21

00-026082

Printed in the United States of America
First Edition

To my brother David—always the scientist.

Contents

Carl Sagan

(Photograph by Bill Ray, courtesy of Ann Druyan.)

Chapter One

Star Gazing

When Carl Sagan was seven years old he wanted to know more about stars. His parents had told him that they were just little lights in the night sky, but he still had questions. What kind of light? Why were they there? What were they made of?

Determined to find an answer to his question, Carl took a streetcar to the New Utrecht, Brooklyn, branch of the New York Public Library to check out his first science book. But, when he asked the librarian for a book on stars, she gave him one about *movie* stars. He tried again, explaining that he wanted a book about the stars in the sky, about *astronomy*. The librarian found the right book this time, and Carl read it in one sitting. He discovered that each star was not just a bright light but was a potential sun. "This just blew my mind. Until then the universe had been my neighborhood," Carl said later.

Carl began visiting the library more and more to satisfy

his ever-growing curiosity. For the first time he realized just how big the Universe would have to be. There must be planets revolving around other suns. He wondered if there were life on those planets.

Carl's fascination with science had begun early. When he was five, his parents took him to the 1939 New York World's Fair, which offered a vision of a streamlined "World of Tomorrow." At one exhibit Carl actually "saw" sound. A machine called an *oscilloscope* displayed the sound waves made when a tuning fork was struck by a hammer. At another exhibit he "heard" light when a flashlight was shone on a photocell. The light on the cell produced static which sounded something like a radio that is not properly tuned.

Carl Edward Sagan was born in the Bensonhurst section of Brooklyn, New York, on November 9, 1934. His father, Samuel, worked as a garment cutter in a ladies' coat factory. Samuel had emigrated from the Ukraine when he was five years old. Carl's mother, Rachel, was born in the United States to Austrian Jewish parents. After the early death of her mother, she was shuttled back to Europe to live with aunts. When her father remarried, he sent for his daughter to return to New York. Samuel and Rachel met at a party in Brooklyn. On March 14, 1933, they were married. Carl was their first child. His sister, Carol, was born when he was seven.

Young Carl Sagan skipped several grades at P.S. 101.
(Courtesy of Ann Druyan.)

Carl's elementary school, P.S. (Public School) 101, informed Samuel and Rachel that their gifted son might benefit from a private school. Although they were proud of Carl's ability, lack of money prevented them from sending him to private school. He skipped several grades instead. Samuel and Rachel provided as many opportunities for their bright son as they could afford. When money was particularly scarce, Samuel ushered at a movie theater to make ends meet. On the weekends the family often visited museums together. Sometimes they went to the Hayden Planetarium.

In addition to his public education, Carl received a religious education at his temple's Hebrew school. While his father was not a believer, his mother was devout and attended the temple on a regular schedule. As Carl grew, the ideas he learned in Hebrew school and the science he learned through his own reading seemed to be in conflict. Carl grew skeptical of his family's religious tradition.

One night after dinner, Samuel presented Carl with this mathematical principle: a number can always be made bigger. Intrigued, Carl wrote "1 + 1 = 2" on a gray cardboard shirt form his father had brought home from the coat factory. Then he wrote, "2 + 1 = 3" and so on. Carl decided he would add 1 to every number up to 1,000. He excitedly wrote out his answers, using more and more sheets of gray cardboard, until Rachel told him he had to take a bath. Samuel promised to continue the addition while Carl was in the tub. Well into the night, father and son finally reached 1,001.

Carl decided he wanted to do "science," but he was unsure how. No one in his family believed you could actually make money as a scientist. His parents assumed that he would follow his father's footsteps in the garment industry. Carl resigned himself to having a regular job when he grew up and pursuing science on the weekends and evenings.

By the time he was eight, Carl had read his fair share of science and science fiction. One of his favorite science-fiction writers was Edgar Rice Burroughs. Burroughs wrote fantastic tales about space travel and green Martians, beautiful princesses in distress and spired cities on faraway planets. His stories had an extraordinary effect on Carl's imagination. Even though Carl knew how far away Mars really was from studying astronomy books, he once stood on a hillside and implored the Martians to beam him up.

Astounding Science Fiction magazine found its way to Carl's bookshelf, too. These stories were more scientifically accurate than Burroughs's. During World War II, he heard about the V-2 rockets the Germans used to rain death and destruction on Britain. Put to peaceful uses, Carl reasoned that these rockets would be a far better way to get to Mars than Burroughs's fantasy travel.

The story in *Astounding* that affected him the most was one about an atomic bomb. When Carl read the story, World War II was raging in the Pacific. The war would end when the United States dropped atomic bombs on the Japanese cities of Hiroshima and Nagasaki.

Carl was lucky that his parents helped him learn more about science because at school he could not count on his teachers. In elementary school he memorized the Periodic Table of the Elements and learned about levers and inclined planes, photosynthesis, and the difference between anthracite and bituminous coal. But none of his teachers ever put these facts and phenomena into context. Long division was nothing more than a set of rules; the teachers never explained how the right answer was produced. Carl never found his excitement about science reflected in the classroom. Evolution was not even mentioned. "School was little more than a detention camp," Carl said later.

Not long after the end of the war, Carl read the great science-fiction writers H. G. Wells and Jules Verne. He found he was growing tired of make-believe. Carl yearned for real science. When his grandfather asked him what he wanted to be when he grew up, Carl replied, "An astronomer." His grandfather came back with the old refrain, "Yes, but how will you make your living?" Carl still had no answer.

The science fiction of H. G. Wells inspired Carl to learn more about astronomy.
(Courtesy of the University of Illinois Library at Urbana-Champaign.)

The very next year, in 1947, Samuel was promoted to manager of the coat factory. The family could afford to live in a nicer neighborhood, and they moved to the suburbs across the Hudson River in Rahway, New Jersey.

At Rahway High, things failed to improve for Carl. He took courses that required laboratory work, but found them too easy. Math class was equally dull. When it came time to extract square roots, Carl quickly learned the formula and plugged in the right answers. At Rahway, students were discouraged from following their own ideas. The material that interested Carl the most was at the school library in books that never got assigned. Carl read as much as he could on his own.

Carl made one "scientific" discovery at Rahway High. He learned from his biology teacher that astronomers actually got paid. "The idea that I could be a professional astronomer, that there was such a thing, that they paid you enough to have three square meals and spend all your time studying this stuff—that was a glorious discovery."

When sixteen-year-old Carl graduated in the spring of 1951, his school yearbook named him "most likely to succeed" and "the class brains." With his top grades he could consider a variety of good colleges. While other schools bragged about their athletic teams or fraternity life, the emphasis placed on academics in a University of Chicago brochure caught Carl's attention. At Chicago, he could study the humanities—literature, history, and art—as well as science. Once University of Chicago officials assured Carl that an engineering degree was unnecessary to fly spaceships to other planets, he enrolled as an undergraduate.

Chapter Two

Chicago

When Carl arrived in Chicago in the fall of 1951, his older cousin Bruce Sagan was there to greet him. Bruce guided Carl through the University of Chicago campus and listened with amazement as his sixteen-year-old cousin discussed left-handed particles with another student. Bruce had no idea what they were talking about.

Carl found the University of Chicago congenial to his ambitions. The university was home to Nobel Prize-winner Enrico Fermi. Beneath the football stands in December 1942, as part of the secret war time effort to build an atomic bomb, Fermi had set off the first controlled chain nuclear reaction.

Robert Maynard Hutchins, who stepped down as president the year Carl arrived, had completely reorganized the university's curriculum during the 1930s to reflect his concern with what he called the "Great Books." Hutchins believed that students should get to know the most important thinkers of the past by reading their work, rather than by relying on what some textbook said about their ideas.

At sixteen, Carl was reading Plato and John Stuart Mill, Sophocles and Dostoyevsky. He and his fellow students were required to respond to what they had read. "It was unthinkable for an aspiring physicist not to know Aristotle, Bach, Shakespeare, Malinowski and Freud. In an introductory science class, Ptolemy's view that the Sun revolved around the Earth was presented so compellingly that some students found themselves reevaluating their commitment to Copernicus," he said later. Carl, at 6' 2", was also the captain of a championship intramural basketball team. He was known for his aggressive rebounding and sharp elbows.

After his freshman year, Carl landed a job as a student researcher. During summer break, he worked at Indiana University under the Nobel Prize-winning biologist Hermann Muller. Muller was researching the origins of life. Carl's job was to raise the fruit flies that Muller used in his experiments. The job was not particularly glamorous, but Carl found that he and his boss had two important things in common: A love for science fiction and the belief in life on other planets. Muller taught Carl that he needed to study biology if he wanted to understand life on other worlds.

Upon leaving for Chicago at the end of the summer, Muller provided Carl with a letter of introduction to another Nobel Prize-winner, Harold Urey. Urey was a chemist at the University of Chicago whose experiments on the origin of life were becoming well known. He and a graduate student named Stanley Miller were testing their hypothesis that life began when naturally occurring simple compounds (like carbon dioxide and water) were zapped by lightning on primordial Earth. The electricity caused these simple compounds to form into more complex organic compounds, and these organic compounds then transmuted into what we know as Life. The Miller-Urey experiment produced amino acids, the building blocks of proteins. When Carl's sophomore year began that fall, he signed up for chemistry courses with Harold Urey and introduced himself to Stanley Miller.

Carl kept a logbook of observations he made through the university's telescope during his sophomore year. What he mostly saw through Chicago's cloudy skies was *rien*, French for "nothing," as he wrote in one entry. Most of the time he reported that he had spent his time studying because there was nothing to see. He tried to watch an eclipse with friends on the afternoon of January 29, 1953, but the viewing, he wrote, was "snowed under!"

After two years studying the classics, Carl received his Associate's degree and was faced with choosing a major.

Although his research with Muller drew him toward biology, and his exposure to Urey pointed to chemistry, Carl prudently settled on physics. In 1955 he received his Bachelor's of Science and a year later, his Master's. Physics proved an excellent foundation for his post-graduate study of astronomy.

Carl spent the summer of 1956 at the McDonald Observatory at Fort Davis, Texas. He worked for planetary astronomer Gerard Kuiper observing Mars. Kuiper supported the hypothesis that Mars was a life-sustaining planet, marked by deep canals and melting polar ice caps. He believed that Mars was covered with thick patches of low-growing lichens and moss. When Carl got his first chance to view the Red Planet, he was disappointed. Through the telescope, it seemed a small, yellowish disk, void of *anything*.

Carl spent his free time that summer driving his second-hand station wagon to visit his girlfriend Lynn Alexander. Carl and Lynn had met at the University of Chicago campus. She was a liberal arts major who had entered the university early, like Carl. Their relationship was tempestuous, yet they still spoke of marriage. Carl's mother, Rachel, wondered what her son saw in Lynn.

That fall, Carl accepted a position at the University of Chicago astronomy school's Yerkes Observatory in Williams Bay, Wisconsin, under Subrahmanyan Chandrasekhar.

Chandra, as he was called, was a mathematical genius. Carl found his attention to detail admirable, but preferred Kuiper's estimations that quickly linked idea to idea. "It was from Kuiper that I got a feeling for what is called a back-of-the-envelope calculation: A possible explanation to a problem occurs to you, you pull out an old envelope, appeal to your knowledge of fundamental physics, scribble a few approximate equations on the envelope, substitute in likely numerical values, and see if your answer comes anywhere near explaining your problem. If not, you look for a different explanation. It cut through nonsense like a knife through butter." Carl was much more interested in piecing together large concepts rather than fooling around with minute details.

Carl's talent for publicizing science began to show itself in 1957 when he organized a successful campus lecture series. "The Creation of Life and the Universe" became standing-room-only events. Carl invited lecturers and even gave one talk himself. Not all of the faculty were thrilled with what they saw as popularization and grandstanding. A disgruntled teacher called it "Sagan's Circus." Other faculty members criticized Carl for promoting scientific research to the public. One teacher took him aside and observed disapprovingly, "I've been following your career in the *New York Times*."

Carl's reputation grew at the university for having

Carl studied at the University of Chicago through the post-graduate level.

(Photograph by Jim Hughes for The Christian Science Monitor, *courtesy of Ann Druyan.)*

unusual scientific interests. While other astronomers were preoccupied with the stars, Carl was concerned with the planets and their ability to sustain life. Carl published his first paper in a 1956 volume of *Evolution* called "Radiation and the Origin of the Gene." His interest in exobiology, the study of the possibility of life on other worlds, was at that time out of favor. "The idea of going to other planets, even the idea of studying other planets, was considered by many astronomers disreputable, fatally compromised by Percival Lowell," Carl later said. (Lowell was the Massachusetts astronomer who had dedicated his life to studying the later-discredited "canals" of Mars.)

Carl's belief in life on other planets would not cause him to skew his findings. In December of 1956, at the age of twenty-two, Carl gave his first scientific paper at the American Association for the Advancement of Science in New York. While Kuiper still supported that vegetation grew on Mars, Carl's ideas had changed. His observations at the Texas observatory revealed there were *no* seasonal color changes on the Martian surface, especially in the greens and blues that Kuiper thought indicated plant life. This meant that color variations were only optical illusions. They failed as solid evidence for the existence of plants. Carl proposed that wind was the source of seasonal color changes on Mars, even though his hypothesis was a case against exobiology.

Carl and Lynn were married on June 16, 1957. Lynn was nineteen and Carl, twenty-two. Rachel still did not approve of her son's choice. Lynn had begun studying genetics, and that summer the newlyweds worked and studied at the University of Colorado. In the fall they planned to return to Wisconsin where Lynn would begin her graduate work at the University of Wisconsin at Madison, and Carl could work at the Yerkes Observatory.

In Madison, Carl befriended Nobel Prize-winning geneticist Joshua Lederberg. Each man was impressed by the other's mastery of his field and each tutored the other on his own specialty. They regularly discussed their ideas about extraterrestrial life. But, Lederberg had accepted a position at Stanford University. He left for California shortly after he and Carl met.

In October 1957, the Soviet Union sent the first man-made object into space, a satellite called *Sputnik*, or "little traveler." *Sputnik* was made of metal, the size and shape of a basketball. It sent out simple radio signals. Carl found *Sputnik* an inspiration, and he bet a classmate a box of chocolate bars (his favorite food) that there would be a man on the moon by 1970.

It was a good time to be doing science. *Sputnik* prompted the U.S. government to pour money into scientific research. The National Aeronautics and Space Administration (NASA) was hiring and, following Joshua Lederberg's suggestion, took Carl on as a consultant to robotic, or unmanned, missions. Carl and Lynn's first child, Dorion Solomon Sagan, had been born, and the job was a welcome boon. Carl's first major concern was that the space agency sterilize rocket probes and satellites that they would send to the Moon to protect from contaminating extra-terrestrial life with microbes from Earth. Some of Carl's colleagues criticized this idea, arguing it was inconceivable that life existed on the Moon. Carl believed it was conceivable for microbes to exist deep within the lunar surface. NASA was finally convinced. Others wondered if the Soviet Union would be as careful. Sagan approached the Soviet Academy of Sciences, but they evaded his questions.

Carl's Ph.D. dissertation, *Physical Studies of Planets*, incorporated some of the work he had prepared for NASA. He used the data gathered by the rocket probes in laboratory simulations of planetary atmospheres—simulations that would help him to draw conclusions about the nature of dust storms on Mars or the surface temperature on Venus. Working with the NASA data, he calculated Venus was not the habitable planet that so many people thought it was, but was actually a hellishly hot place with a surface temperature of about 900 degrees. He hypothesized that Venus's atmosphere was made up of thick carbon dioxide that trapped heat from the Sun and made life impossible. He called this phenomenon the "greenhouse effect."

The greenhouse effect was important to a debate going on right here on Earth. Although carbon dioxide naturally occurs in our atmosphere, the burning of fossil fuels also produces carbon dioxide (among other substances). This excess carbon dioxide can trigger global warming. According to Carl, "a little greenhouse effect is a good thing"—it traps heat and allows life to develop. But too much—caused by the carbon dioxide produced by burning oil, coal and natural gas—could make Earth too hot to live on. The greenhouse effect and global warming continue to be important environmental concerns today.

In June 1960, Carl earned a Ph.D. in astronomy and astrophysics from the University of Chicago. Lynn was pregnant with their second child. Carl was awarded a fellowship at the University of California at Berkeley after Lederberg's nomination, and the family prepared for the cross-country journey.

Chapter Three

Young Professor

Carl spent two years at the University of California at Berkeley as a Miller Research Fellow in the astronomy department. He resumed his friendship with Joshua Lederberg who worked at nearby Stanford University. He also co-edited his first book, *The Atmospheres of Mars and Venus*. In October 1960, Carl and Lynn's second son, Jeremy Ethan Sagan, was born.

The birth of a child did little to help settle the growing problems in the Sagan household. The stress of trying to juggle parenthood, Carl's new responsibilites, and Lynn's doctoral studies in genetics was too much for the young couple. Their relationship began to show the strain, and they argued frequently.

At Berkeley, Carl's focus was research, but he also taught one class. He published a paper pursuing his research on Venus, suggesting that the next logical step was making the planet habitable for humans—assuming the surface was much like a desert on Earth. To make the planet habitable, Carl envisioned seeding the upper atmosphere of Venus with algae. Algae would be able to derive moisture from water vapor and withstand Venus's strong ultraviolet light and temperatures. The algae would absorb carbon dioxide, reduce the temperature, and produce the oxygen needed for a "micro-biological re-engineering of Venus." Though there has been no attempt to change Venus, his idea of "terra-forming" has appeared in science-fiction movies and novels.

In 1960, Carl was invited by NASA to be an experimenter for the *Mariner* probe. *Mariner* would travel to Venus, becoming the first U. S. mission to another planet. At the age of twenty-seven, he made the first of many appearances on national network television, articulating the importance of the *Mariner* exploration. Shortly after his television appearance, Carl and the rest of the world watched as the probe malfunctioned just after launch and was destroyed. He rejoined NASA for the successful 1962 *Mariner 2* launch. This time, *Mariner 2* sent back data confirming the greenhouse effect.

Frank Drake, an astronomer who had been searching for intelligent life in the universe using radio telescopes, invited Carl to a meeting in Green Bank, West Virginia. The group of eleven men wanted to build support for government financing of the search for extra-terrestrial life. They decided to call themselves CETI (Communication for Extra-Terrestrial Intelligence.)

The first challenge the group met was to make an intelligent estimate of how many possible alien civilizations existed in the Milky Way galaxy. To meet this challenge, Drake developed an equation that is still used today.

In his equation, Frank Drake called the number of extra-terrestrial civilizations *N*. The seven factors that produce *N* are: 1) the rate of star formation, 2) the fraction of stars that have planets, 3) the average number of planets that might contain life in a solar system, 4) the fraction of such planets that actually produce life, 5) the fraction of such planets that produce intelligent life, 6) the fraction of such species that attempt to communicate with intelligent life on other planets, and 7) the lifetime of such communicating planets.

The members of CETI spent most of this first meeting debating the variables of the Drake equation. After two days they decided that the number of intelligent civilizations in the Galaxy was somewhere between 1,000 and 100 million. The factor that caused the most debate was the seventh: How long do intelligent civilizations exist? This question ultimately led the group to speculate on what destroys civilizations. Because of the rapid buildup of nuclear weapons since the end of World War II, this seemed to be the most omnious variable in Drake's equation.

While Carl was grappling with the number of intelligent civilizations elsewhere in the Galaxy, Lynn was breaking new ground in genetics research. She proposed a new theory, "serial endosymbiosis," after studying chloroplasts (the part of a plant cell that contains chlorophyll). Her professor noticed that the chloroplasts looked very similar to blue-green bacteria. Lynn proposed that chloroplasts were once independent bacteria that had evolved symbiotically to live inside plant cells. She tested her hypothesis by matching the DNA of chloroplasts with the DNA of blue-green bacteria. She later proved that mitochondria in animal cells had gone through the same evolution. Her theory has forever changed the field of biology.

In the fall of 1962, Carl was granted an appointment to the Smithsonian Astrophysical Observatory. The same year, Harvard University hired him as an astrophysicist and assistant professor of astronomy. Instead of returning east immediately, he decided to train further in the skills he needed for exobiology at Stanford under his old friend Joshua Lederberg. Carl spent the next year working in Lederberg's genetics laboratory at the Stanford University School of Medicine.

While at Stanford, Carl published an article arguing

that life developed on Earth, attacking a widely-held view that a "space bug" brought life to the planet. He stated that the vast distances and the intense radiation in space would make this kind of travel impossible. Instead he maintained the competing view he had first encountered in the Miller-Urey experiment. Carl pursued experiments anew with his colleagues at Stanford, Cyril Ponnamperuma and Ruth Mariner. They irradiated organic molecules with ultraviolet light in the presence of phosphoric acid, producing small amounts of adenosine triphosphate (ATP), the key energy source in biological systems.

Carl and Lynn finally decided to divorce. At first, Lynn moved with Dorion and Jeremy to Port Richmond, California, but when Carl took up his teaching post at Harvard in 1963, he convinced her to move to Massachusetts with him. The situation would be temporary. Carl, at age twenty-eight, moved from their apartment to nearby Cambridge within a few months.

When Carl arrived at Harvard, he soon garnered a reputation for being an outstanding teacher. He was easily recognized by his penchant for wearing turtleneck sweaters. His views on exobiology also caused him notice at the conservative Ivy League school. Although he had a knack for pulling many scientific disciplines into his lectures, some of his colleagues thought his style of teaching was irresponsible and egotistical.

During his years at Harvard, Carl had two significant experiences that affected his public role as a scientist. The first intensified his (and the U. S.'s) scientific cooperation with the Soviet Union. The second increased his belief that superstition ruled public thinking on science.

Carl was invited to meet some Soviet scientists who were interested in the possibility of extra-terrestrial life. Any dealings with the Soviets were difficult at that time because of the Cold War. Feelings between the United States and the Soviet Union were especially brittle after President Kennedy forced Premier Krushchev to remove Soviet missiles from Cuba.

At the meeting, Carl was introduced to Alexander Imshenetsky, one of three Soviet scientists who were interested in the search for extra-terrestrial life. Also present was a translator from the Library of Congress. The men talked for a few hours before the Soviets had to catch a plane. Later, Carl discovered that the translator was actually an intelligence agent, a spy. This man, who had assumed that Carl was also an American agent, pressed him for the details of his private conversation with Imshenetsky. Carl refused.

Two years later, at an Italian space science conference, Carl ran into Imshenetsky again. In a corner of the room sat the same American spy. There was no doubt that Imshenetsky had known who the American agent was from the beginning. It became clear to Carl that any cooperative efforts between the U.S. and the Soviet Union would mean first overcoming the distrust between the two governments.

In 1964, Carl and another young scientist, Richard Lewontin, traveled to Arkansas at the request of Hermann Muller. Muller asked them to take the affirmative side in a debate titled "Resolved, that the theory of evolution is as proved as is the fact that the Earth goes around the Sun." One of their opponents in the debate was a professor of biology from a fundamentalist college in Texas. Most in the audience were Christians who read the Bible literally. They believed that God had created Earth and all of the animals on it only a few thousand years ago. Despite Carl and his colleague's certainty, the audience sided with the fundamentalists. Carl and Richard Lewontin sneaked out the back door of the auditorium and left town in a hurry. Carl viewed this vivid confrontation between creationism and evolution as a struggle between ignorance and knowledge. It inspired him to continue his assault on ignorance of science.

In 1966, Carl collaborated on what would become a celebrated book with the Soviet Union's leading expert on life on other planets, I. S. Shklovskii. Shklovskii fully believed that there was other intelligent life in the Universe. He proposed that Phobos and Deimos, the potato-shaped moons of Mars, showed signs of being artificial satellites and were possibly remnants of an extinct Martian civilization. Carl had written a paper on the idea of interstellar travel. Taking a chance, he mailed a copy of the paper to Shklovskii. By the time Shklovskii received Carl's paper, the Soviet scientist was preparing to write a book of his own on the same topic. After reading Carl's paper, Shklovskii invited him to contribute to an English translation of his book.

Shklovskii's book, *Intelligent Life in the Universe*, was well received in the Soviet Union. Carl added ten new chapters, more than doubling the original length of the book. The book was a comprehensive treatment of the origin of the Universe, the evolution of the stars and planets, and the beginning of life on Earth. The book laid the groundwork for the continued search for extra-terrestrial intelligence that was begun by Carl's colleague, Frank Drake.

As Carl became more well known to the public, he started to make connections with other famous people. On February 19, 1963, Carl met the famed science-fiction writer Isaac Asimov for lunch. It was the beginning of a lifelong friendship.

Although Carl had dabbled in science-fiction writing, he never acquiesced to the notion that so-called Unidentified Flying Objects, or UFOs, were actually aliens from other worlds. Carl always pointed out that no one had ever provided any hard evidence that UFOs were spaceships. He noted how unlikely it was that aliens would travel to Earth, given the vastness of the distances in the Galaxy and the limitations imposed by the speed of light.

Movies about humans coming into contact with aliens were something else. Director Stanley Kubrick and writer Arthur C. Clarke were making their famous science-fiction film *2001: A Space Odyssey*. They planned to show the aliens as moviegoers would expect. But, after they consulted Carl, they took his suggestion that the aliens never be shown directly—partly because it was impossible to know what they would look like. (Though Kubrick was willing to accept Carl's suggestion for his movie, he was so worried that real aliens would show up while he was making it that he asked the giant insurance company Lloyds of London to insure against "alien contact" during the filming of the movie.)

In July 1965, *Mariner 4* shot photographs of the Martian surface. Carl hoped that the *Mariner 4* exploration would answer the question about life on the planet. The pictures showed a barren, cratered landscape devoid of canals and anything that resembled water or vegetation. Winds swept huge dust storms swirling across the planet's surface. Carl interpreted the findings in a number of articles with his colleague James Pollack.

Carl's life seemed to be moving right along. With the exception of a few faculty members who thought him too egotistical (and the field of exobiology a fly-by-night discipline), he was well liked and respected at Harvard. By 1966, he was also very involved in more social issues, such as speaking out against the Vietnam War and supporting the civil rights movement.

During this time, Carl also met a beautiful young artist named Linda Salzman. Linda was a student at the School of the Museum of Fine Arts in Boston. Soon after they met, the couple moved in together. He and Linda often visited his new friend Lester Grinspoon, a Harvard psychiatrist.

Just as everything seemed to be going smoothly in his life, Carl received a shock. Fred Whipple, the head of the Harvard astronomy department, called Carl into his office and told him that he could not expect to be granted tenure, or the promise of a permanent job, at the university. By denying him tenure, Harvard was telling Carl that he should look elsewhere for a position. In effect, the brilliant young scientist had been rejected by the most prestigious university in the country. To add insult to injury, Whipple did not tell Carl why he had been denied tenure. It was over a decade before Carl discovered that Professor Urey had written a letter criticizing him for the quality of his work.

Chapter Four

In the Public Eye

As soon as Carl learned he would have to leave Harvard, he started to look for another job. He went across town to MIT (Massachusetts Institute of Technology) where he was also rejected. Then, he was contacted by Thomas Gold, the head of the budding astronomy department at Cornell University. The organization that had formed at Green Bank with Frank Drake, Communication for Extra-Terrestrial Intelligence (CETI) was now located at Cornell. The group had changed its name to Search for Extra-Terrestrial Intelligence (SETI).

Thomas Gold wanted Carl in his department. He was impressed by his work and his fame. He offered him an associate professorship with tenure within a few years, but Carl balked. He demanded his own laboratory. Thomas Gold agreed to let Carl open the Laboratory for Planetary Studies.

On April 6, 1968, Carl and Linda married in the MIT

chapel. Lester Grinspoon was Carl's best man and Isaac Asimov was the official witness. After their honeymoon, the couple moved to a rented house in Ithaca, New York.

From the beginning, Carl's classes at Cornell were fully enrolled and his campus lecture series on science drew standing-room-only crowds. Carl used models and simple illustrations to explain the complexities of astronomy, biology, and astrophysics. His students were entertained by the sight of their instructor dancing around—doing a kind of hula, they said—to demonstrate the movement of photons (light particles), a staggered motion that otherwise required complicated math to describe. He made "whoosh" noises to mimic molecules escaping from Earth's atmosphere into space. Carl became the faculty editor of *Icarus*, a journal of the planetary sciences published at the university. In 1970, he was granted tenure.

Only a year after arriving at Cornell, he organized a scientific symposium with Thornton Page in order to encourage serious debate on UFOs. He explained why popular evidence for UFOs was inconclusive. Other members on the panel argued that the hundreds of eyewitness accounts must prove their existence.

Carl was an active contributor to NASA during the next decade. He joined the *Viking 1* and 2 Martian landing site group with Harold Urey and Joshua Lederberg among others. He was invited to be on the briefing team for *Apollo 11*, the spaceship that carried the first men to the moon. As exciting as the prospect was, he had his concerns. He believed that robotic missions performed more cheaply and safely. He also realized the political motivation behind putting humans on the moon: It was designed to capture the attention of the nation *and* the Soviet Union. Most importantly, Carl worried that the astronauts might carry dangerous substances from the lunar surface back to Earth on their clothes and equipment. He encouraged NASA to set up a "back contamination" system that would require the rocket and the astronauts to be quarantined until they were properly cleansed. At first, NASA reluctantly agreed to follow Carl's advice about back contamination.

On July 20, 1969, Neil Armstrong became the first human to walk on the surface of the moon. Carl watched the historical footage from a hospital bed. He had suffered from esophagus trouble since he was a teenager. His esophagus periodically lost the ability to contract and move food down to his stomach, causing inflammation and bleeding. He was recovering from surgery when *Apollo* landed. Carl later learned that NASA had failed to comply with the back contamination procedures he had organized when *Apollo* and its crew returned to Earth.

The 1969 launches of *Mariner 6* and *7* brought back

While consulting NASA on various missions during the 1970s, Carl continued to be a popular teacher at Cornell.

(Photograph by Meyerowitz for Scientific American*, courtesy of Ann Druyan.)*

pictures of the ice caps on the Martian poles. Although the ice caps were once thought to be made of water, the *Mariner* studies proved them to be carbon dioxide. *Mariner 9* was significant in another way, too. When the spacecraft first landed, its view was blocked for three months by a giant, planet-wide dust storm. Though that storm ended and *Mariner* sent back photographs for a year, the larger significance of a giant dust storm that heated the atmosphere and cooled the surface would become clear to Carl over a decade later, when scientists began to debate the possibility of what became known as "nuclear winter."

Carl was optimistic about the possibility of life elsewhere. He thought that life could even exist on Jupiter, although it would have to be very different from the life we know if it were going to survive on the gaseous giant. He speculated that there could be creatures composed largely of gas that floated freely in the Jovian atmosphere. But for all his speculation, Carl never left the verifiable world for very long. In September 1970, he and Linda's first son, Nicholas Julian Zapata Sagan, was born. In 1971, he was honored to write the entry on "Life" in the *Encyclopedia Britannica*.

In March 1972, *Pioneer 10* was launched toward Jupiter. Its final destination was the asteroid belt beyond our solar system. *Pioneer* instruments would send back

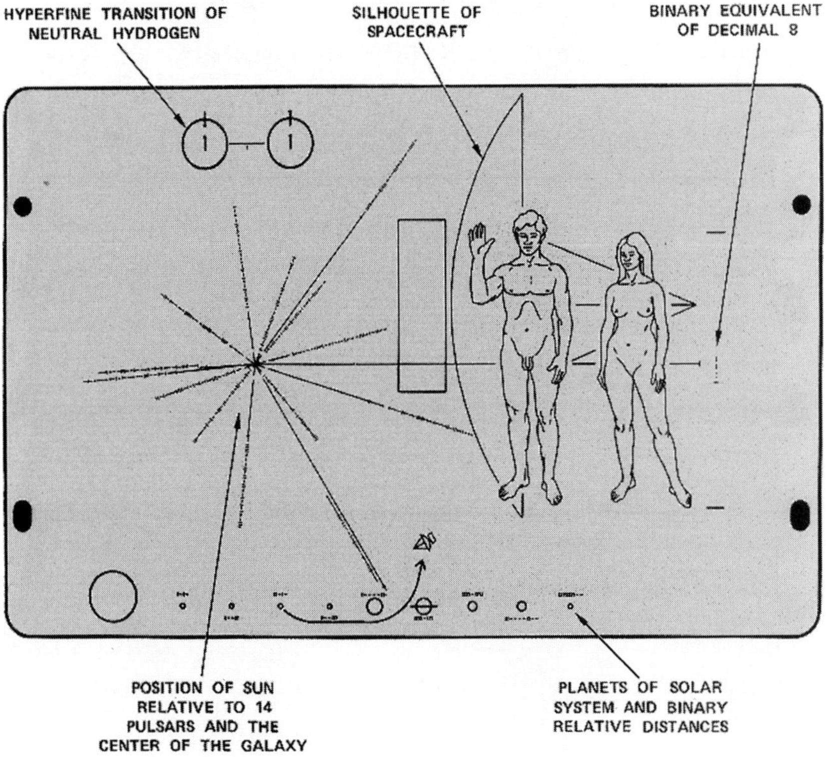

The *Pioneer* plaque included information about Earth's location and the appearance of human beings.

information as it passed Jupiter and the other planets. *Pioneer* also carried a special passenger: A golden plaque designed by Carl, Linda, and Frank Drake.

It was Carl who had suggested the plaque to NASA. The plaque contained information about Earth and the human race. It would drift through the Galaxy for hundreds of millions of years—or until space-faring aliens stopped the probe and read the plaque. Carl and Frank worked out the message in just a few hours in December 1971. Because the aliens could not be expected to understand English or any other language, the gold-anodized aluminum plate contained "universals"—a drawing of a hydrogen atom, a map of our solar system in the Galaxy with the spacecraft emerging from the third planet, and renditions of a nude man and woman drawn by Linda.

An identical plate was put on *Pioneer 11* when it was launched in 1973. Pictures of the plate appeared in newspapers and magazines all over the world—sometimes with the nude people covered up. For millions of people, the plaque brought home the idea of possible contact by our species with aliens. When the nude drawings were denounced as "smut," Carl used the controversy to campaign for more missions. Some people had a very different concern about nude drawings. Were we giving away our position to hostile aliens, they asked? Not, answered Carl, if they already picked up radio and

TV broadcasts heading out through the Galaxy at the speed of light.

During this period, Carl became a television star. In 1972, he made the first of twenty-five appearances on the *Tonight Show*. The host, Johnny Carson, asked him about the existence of UFOs, and Carl said that he did not believe in them, not because they could not exist, but because there was no evidence for them.

UFO enthusiasts found it hard to believe that a man who thought that there was intelligent life elsewhere in the Universe could deny that any of those life forms had traveled to Earth.

The problem was that the only "evidence" for UFOs was strange eye-witness stories. There were reports of eerie lights, aliens themselves, or abduction. Still, there had never been any actual evidence of a spaceship. To Carl, this meant that people were hallucinating, dreaming, or lying.

The sheer vastness of space and the unlikelihood that any alien civilization would have heard of us, much less have been able to come here, made alien sightings even harder to believe. Some UFO enthusiasts argued that "Chariots of the Gods" myths really referred to ancient astronauts, who had been mistaken for gods and had given rise to civilization, or even life, on Earth. But, as Carl noted, there was no evidence for the "Chariots" theory.

His second appearance on the *Tonight Show*, three weeks later, cemented Carl's popularity. Other guests would talk about their latest movie, book, or concert. But, Carl was different. "Fifteen billion years ago the Universe was without form. There were no galaxies, stars, or planets. There was no life. There was darkness everywhere," he intoned. Carl gave a history of the Universe on a late-night TV talk show, in fifteen minutes, to several million people. Surely some of those viewers were young people trying to decide what to do with their lives. If they had not previously considered becoming astronomers, they might now.

The *Tonight Show* made him a celebrity. He attracted autograph hunters and swooning women. Besides his appearances on Carson's show, he hosted science programs for the British Broadcasting Corporation and was interviewed extensively by major newspapers and national magazines. "My only secret in being able to talk to others about science is to remember what it was like when I didn't understand whatever it was we were talking about," he said.

The name "Carl Sagan" soon became a household word. The same year, Carl was interviewed by Timothy Ferris of *Rolling Stone*. During his stays in New York City, Carl enjoyed visiting Ferris and his fiancé, Ann Druyan. He published another book for non-scientists,

The Cosmic Connection: An Extraterrestrial Perspective, a series of essays on the possibility of encountering alien intelligence.

The Cosmic Connection sold well because Carl knew how to write about science with poetry and passion. His writing was livelier than the usual scientific treatise. He recalled his childhood fascination with Mars, tying Edgar Rice Burroughs-style fantasy to his descriptions of *Mariner 9*'s first images of the two tiny Martian satellites, Phobos and Deimos. The moons, which resembled pockmarked potatoes, were so tiny (Phobos, the larger of the two, is less than nine miles long) and their gravity so slight that an astronaut standing on their surfaces could easily pitch a baseball into orbit. He also called for international collaboration in space exploration, although the U. S. and the Soviet Union were frozen in the midst of the Cold War.

Chapter Five

Searching the Heavens

In 1971, Carl and Frank Drake attempted to make contact by sending signals out into the vastness of space from the giant radio telescope at Cornell University's Arecibo Observatory in Puerto Rico.

Frank and Carl set the radio telescope to emit the frequency of hydrogen, 1420 MHz, as a base reading. Any artifical signal from space, they reasoned, would alter the frequency. They would chart the changes on an oscilloscope. They aimed the telescope at a giant cluster of stars in the Andromeda galaxy.

After 100 hours of observation, the men had to give up. Carl took this failure especially hard. He had anticipated their chances were very good for encountering some kind of alteration in the signal. He returned to the new home he and Linda had designed in Ithaca. Carl was not alone, however, in his disappointment. After hearing the results of the Arecibo experiment, the Soviet scientist I. S.

Shklovskii concluded cynically that the reason they had not made contact was because all intelligent civilizations eventually blow themselves up in a nuclear war.

Late winter 1974 provided Carl with a chance to refute a fellow scientist's claim about the solar system. In his book *Worlds in Collision,* Soviet psychiatrist Immanuel Velikovsky claimed that Mars once roamed about the solar system before settling in its present-day orbit. He proposed that a giant comet had emerged from Jupiter, passing closely by Earth before locking into orbit around the Sun. The comet, Velikovsky claimed, is Venus. The near-miss had supposedly caused Earth's rotation to slow, causing many of the events reported in the Bible, such as Joshua's claim that the sun had stood still, and Moses's parting of the Red Sea. Although astronomy was not his field, Velikovsky was trying to prove that such Biblical stories had a scientific basis. Carl showed that by its very nature, Venus could not have emerged from Jupiter, thus disproving Velikovsky's argument.

On August 20, 1974, *Viking 1* blasted off for Mars, followed shortly by *Viking 2*. The probes would send landers to the surface (to a site that Carl would help select) while an orbiter continued to circle above the planet. The landing of *Viking 1* was scheduled for July 4, 1976—the U.S. bicentennial. Carl and his family had flown to Florida to watch the launch.

For most of the next year, the Sagans lived in Pasadena, California, so that Carl could work on the *Viking* landing project. They shared an apartment with Carl's oldest son, Dorion, and the engaged couple Timothy Ferris and Ann Druyan. After a series of setbacks, the *Viking* landing was rescheduled for July 20. The first color pictures the lander sent back were of a dark red planet with a pink sky. The lander was also equipped to make life-detecting experiments. A soil sample found no trace of organic compounds. Other experiments were more ambiguous. The *Viking* mission would not yield definite answers to the "life on Mars" debate. Carl noted *not* finding life was important, because it raised the question of why two similar planets differed in this crucial aspect.

Carl was invited by the project manager of the *Voyager 1* and *2* probes in 1976 to produce a message similar to the *Pioneer* plaque. *Voyager* would fly past the outermost planets and their moons, ejecting the message out of the solar system and into the Universe. Ann Druyan was the creative director of the project. Ann, Linda, Timothy Ferris, and Carl worked closely together collecting music, art, and sounds from nature for the *Voyager* record.

The samples were recorded onto gold-plated copper phonograph records. They designed a cover that included a diagram showing how to play them. The records, titled "The Sounds of Earth," carried greetings in sixty lan-

Carl worked with NASA officials to help determine the *Viking 1* and *2* landing site.

guages ranging from Akkadian to Welsh, and contained comments from U. N. Secretary General Kurt Waldheim and President Jimmy Carter ("We hope someday, having solved the problems we face, to join a community of galactic civilizations.")

The earthly sounds included ninety minutes of music from cultures around the world, ranging from Western classical to Eastern classical to tribal music to rock 'n' roll. There was the Chuck Berry classic "Johnny B. Goode," the sound of laughter, of whales at play, and of an automobile shifting gears. Volcanoes rumbled, waves crashed, animal's "spoke." There were video images of the Toronto Airport and rush hour in Calcutta. The human nervous system was explained and a map gave the precise location of the planet Earth. There were 116 photographs of people from all over the world.

Ann Druyan had volunteered to have her heartbeat and brain electrical activity recorded for the *Voyager* record. While the computer recorded, Ann concentrated on the most important questions she could think of: The history of Earth and its life, the history of ideas and human social organization, violence and poverty. And, she also thought about what it was like to fall in love.

Carl and Ann had been attracted to one another since their first meeting. It was not until the creation of the *Voyager* records, that they confided their feelings to one

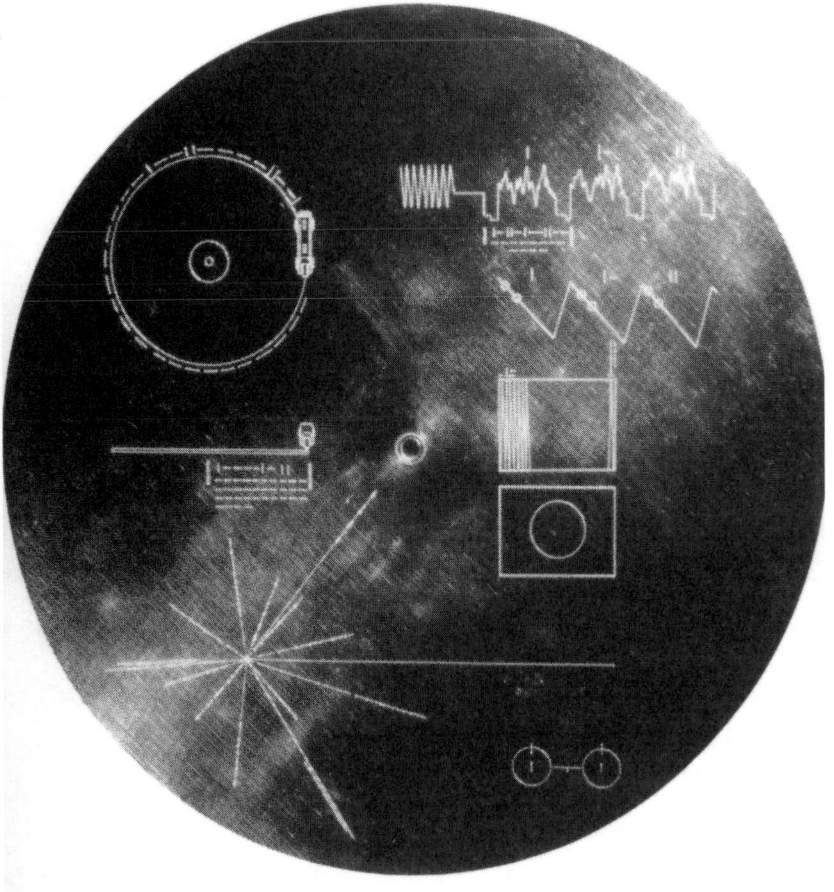

The *Voyager* record cover gave instructions showing how to play the discs.

another. For Ann, "The revelation of being in love with each other was like the discovery of a scientific truth. It was like Eureka, it was like Archimedes." They decided to wait until after the launch to tell Linda and Timothy Ferris.

Carl called the disk "a message in a bottle, thrown into the cosmic ocean." It might "float" for a long time. Engineers predicted that the recordings could last a billion years—long enough for the Earth's continents to drift into wholly new patterns. The *Voyager* is the fastest—and outermost—craft ever created by humans. "It was conceivable," Carl thought, "that we were assembling the ark of human culture, the only artifact that would survive into the unimaginably far distant future."

On August 22, two days after the *Voyager* launch, Carl and Linda arrived at the Grinspoons' home on Cape Cod. Lester had suggested that Carl tell his wife that he had fallen in love with another woman in their presence. She did not take the news well. They argued through the night while Nick slept in another room.

Carl wanted the split with Linda to be amicable; Linda, however, was bitter. She understandably felt betrayed. Eventually, the divorce became a fight over property and child support. But, despite any regrets he may have had about the end of his second marriage, Carl was determined to not let anything stand between spending the rest of his life with Ann, who felt the same way. The couple was now inseparable.

Later in 1977, Carl once again confronted Hollywood's view of aliens and outer space. He had seen the newly-released *Star Wars*, and in November, he sat in a movie theater in New York watching *Close Encounters of the Third Kind*, director Steven Spielberg's fictional treatment of UFOs. Spielberg had carefully loaded his film with every bit of UFO lore. Navy fighter planes mysteriously lost in 1945 showed up without their pilots. Ordinary people became obsessed with finding aliens, even as humanoid aliens abducted some of them. Spacecraft zipped around at ground level and hovered just overhead.

The audience around Carl gaped and gasped. Spielberg's movie had caught their imaginations. But, Carl scoffed. "There's not a smidgen of evidence to suggest that lights in the sky or the disappearance of ships or planes are due to extra-terrestrial intervention."

To Carl, who was constantly being pressured by tabloid reporters to confirm the existence of aliens, the extraterrestrials in Hollywood movies were unlikely simply because the odds against their looking anything like people were so great. They would probably look nothing like human beings even if they were made of the same elements, because the process of carbon and hydrogen evolving into life was so random.

Human beings, he said, had come about as sort of an accident when a cosmic ray hit a gene 4.5 million years ago. The gene mutated and evolved into plants, animals, and eventually humans. "Most biologists," he added, "would agree that if you started the earth over again and merely let the same random factors operate, you would never wind up with anything looking like a human being. If that's the case, then some very different physical planet would have zero chance of producing the aliens you see in the movie."

He also wondered why the producers of the two films had neglected to hire a scientist to guard against scientific inaccuracies. In *Star Wars*, pilot Han Solo shoots into hyperspace at so many "parsecs"—which is a measurement of distance, not speed.

Still, if *Star Wars* and *Close Encounters* excited the imaginations of eight-year-old future scientists, as Burroughs had excited his, then Hollywood might be performing a service after all. And, he had to admit that the main idea in *Close Encounters,* that humans and aliens would communicate by music, made sense.

That same year, Carl published *The Dragons of Eden: Speculations on the Evolution of Human Intelligence,* which won him the Pulitzer Prize. The book grew out of his long-standing interest in the anatomy and physiology of the brain, even though he was not an expert on those subjects. He assumed things that not all scientists and philosophers would agree with—that the brain improves its operation by a kind of evolutionary process, and that our "minds" are merely the operation of our brains. Going even further out on a limb, he speculated that our genes store "memories" of our distant ancestors. He wondered why people sleep and why they dream. He asked, What moral obligations do we have to animals with brains similar to ours—whales and dolphins and apes? And why are apes not able to talk?

The success of *The Dragons of Eden* re-affirmed Carl's belief that people were hungry for scientific knowledge. He had long felt that science was something that anyone should be able to understand and even do. His enthusiasm for popularizing science had made him a controversial figure among the more restrained confines of academia. Carl didn't care. He wanted young people to experience a sense of wonder about science. People should understand why science is a good thing.

In 1976, Carl and a colleague from *Viking* created Carl Sagan Productions, Inc. They planned to use the company to make educational media productions. His first project turned out to be one of the most memorable television events in history. With KCET, the Los Angeles Public Television station, he embarked on the most elaborate project of his career, the thirteen-part series *Cosmos*.

Between 1977 and 1980, Carl, Ann Druyan, and their friend Steven Soter worked on *Cosmos* with dozens of crew members. Carl took a two-year leave of absence from his teaching position at Cornell and moved to Los Angeles with Ann. It was a time of intense work and stress. Adding to the pressure, the family found out that Samuel Sagan had lung cancer. Carl and Ann invited his parents to move from their Florida home and live with them.

The series eventually won three Emmy awards and a Peabody award. *Cosmos* was filmed all over the world, in twelve countries and sixty locations, with the crew often working twenty-hour days. Death Valley stood in for Mars in an illustration of the *Viking* lander's operation. The crew went to Cambridge, England; south India; Egypt; and the Greek island of Samos.

"The cosmos is all that is or ever was or ever will be," Carl declared in his opening narrative. Carl traversed the universe in his imaginary "spaceship of the mind." He used familiar devices to present unfamiliar concepts. He rode a motor scooter around an Italian village to simulate traveling at the speed of light. Through the magic of special effects, he slid down a black hole and strolled through a human brain with electrical impulses flashing all around him. He returned to his old Brooklyn grade school for a lecture on the stars and planets. He walked on a "cosmic calendar" which revealed how little time humans have been on Earth since it formed from cosmic dust 5 billion years ago. He reasoned that if the "Big Bang" started the Universe on January 1, then humans have been around since the last ten seconds of December 31. Carl walked through the Great Library at Alexandria, Egypt, examining historic scrolls—even though the library actually burned to the ground more than 2,000 years ago. He described the important philosophical and mathematical texts that had been lost forever.

Cosmos made its debut on September 28, 1980. The series was entertaining, accurate, and thorough, much like Carl's astronomy lectures at Cornell. Now the whole world could enjoy what his students had enjoyed. Carl was charming and at ease before the camera. He was careful not to confuse fact with speculation. He spoke clearly about complicated subjects, and he made science fun. He hoped that *Cosmos* might help to improve the public's opinion of science and make them more willing to spend tax money on it.

Some in the scientific community criticized the show. They became angry that Carl spoke so fluently about many different areas of science, considering he was not an expert in them all. They said he was "cheapening" real science with oversimplification and making errors to boot. But, he had been careful, and the charges proved weak. Other scientists admired his ability to communicate about what they did. They were pleased by his commitment to take sides in scientific controversies.

Johnny Carson could not resist teasing him on the *Tonight Show*. He impersonated him saying "billions and billions" in a portentous way. Carl said he never actually used that phrase—"it's too imprecise." He claimed not to be bothered by the mimics and the jokesters who poked fun at him, reasoning that if he wanted to avoid being satirized and teased, he needed to stay out of public life.

At the height of his fame from *Cosmos,* Carl and Linda's divorce was finalized. On June 1, 1981, Carl and Ann married at the Hotel Bel-Air in Los Angeles. The wedding was a gala affair. This time, Carl's mother, Rachel, approved of the bride. His father, Samuel, was absent from the celebration. He had died during the creation of *Cosmos*, on October 7, 1979.

Chapter Six

Life Partners

Carl and Ann bought the Sphinx Head Tomb when they returned to Ithaca. The remodeled late-nineteenth century house sat on the edge of a gorge overlooking Ithaca's beautiful Lake Cayuga. Except for the years working on *Cosmos,* Carl was never away from the Cornell campus for long, though he continued to travel constantly.

His third marriage proved a success. Ann became his true partner. They lived and worked together with ease. They were excited by each other's ideas, and their love formed a special bond between them. Ann urged Carl to reacquaint himself with his sons, and she made an effort to befriend them herself.

Carl continued to do scientific research, often with the data from the space probes, as he wrote his popular books and appeared on TV and at symposia. Carl and Ann coauthored several books—*Murmurs of Earth: The Voy-*

ager Interstellar Record, Comet, and *Shadows of Forgotten Ancestors: A Search for Who We Are.* Ann encouraged his social activism.

Carl had been able to create so complex a program as *Cosmos* because he had always been a voracious reader (he would read almost a book a night and remember it all) and a prolific writer. "I like to do diverse things," he said, "in part because if you're doing several things at once, if you get stuck on one, go on to the next. And then you find when you go back to the one you were stuck on, your unconscious mind has made enormous progress while you weren't looking." He did not so much "write" his books as dictate them into a tape recorder for somebody else to type. Ann was the first to read his drafts.

Carl always, as he said, left himself time for "something that makes no sense at all. Every night no matter what, for instance, Annie and I always leave room for five good games of pinochle." He enjoyed scuba diving, table tennis, stamp collecting, and reading for pleasure, especially science and history. He enjoyed relaxing with his family, watching New York Knicks basketball games, going to a movie, and listening to rock music, especially the band Dire Straits. In November 1984, he became a grandfather. Dorion's wife, Marjorie, gave birth to Tonio Jerome Sagan.

Carl's inquisitive nature was always at work, as one

incident vividly revealed. One day the doorbell rang. An exterminator had stopped by to spray for carpenter ants. Carl questioned the man: "What are you spraying? What chemical? You know its structure? You know its chemical formula?" The exterminator gave the name of a chemical. "That's just a name," Carl said. "You have a structural diagram of the molecule?" The exterminator had to produce a diagram before Carl would allow him to spray the house.

As the new decade dawned, the launch of the first space shuttle, *Columbia*, worried Carl that NASA had given up exploring other planets in favor of manned orbits of Earth. In 1980, with no new planetary missions being planned, he founded the Planetary Society. The society would lobby for the continued exploration of the solar system and the search for extraterrestrial life. It would also promote cooperation among nations attempting to explore space.

Meanwhile the battle to continue government funding for SETI was unending. In 1982 Carl rushed to Washington, D.C., to defend the program after Senator William Proxmire tried to cut it from the Federal budget. After an intense private conversation, he managed to persuade the senator to end his criticism. Then he won public backing from seventy world-renowned scientists, including seven Nobel Prize laureates.

In February 1982, Rachel Sagan died. Carl and his mother had always been very close. Some thought he had gotten many of his traits from her. He was very sad at her death. Carl and Ann had their first child, Alexandra Rachel Druyan Sagan, in November of that year. Her parents gave her the nickname "Sasha."

A debate over nuclear winter began at NASA after Luis and Walter Alvarez published an article in 1980 proposing that the dinosaurs were destroyed after Earth was struck by a massive asteroid. This theory suggested that the damage caused by the impact raised such immense clouds of smoke and debris that the sunlight was blocked long enough to create winter-like conditions. As the severe winter continued, the food supply died and the dinosaurs starved or died of exposure. As a result of the article, NASA began testing the phenomenon. One of the questions the researchers asked was "How comparable would the damage be that resulted from an all out nuclear exchange between the United States and the Soviet Union? Would the damage be severe enough to alter the earth's climate?" Some of the data gathered from the *Mariner 9* 1970s exploration of Martian dust storms was reanalyzed in light of the question of the effects of nuclear war. In June 1982, Carl was invited to help evaluate NASA's findings.

Carl appeared on a TV panel discussion with former

In Ann, Carl had found his life's partner.
(Photograph by Tony Korody, courtesy of Ann Druyan.)

secretary of state Henry Kissinger, conservative political columnist William F. Buckley, Jr., and Jewish Holocaust refugee Elie Wiesel immediately after the broadcast of *The Day After* in 1983. The television movie fictionalized a nuclear war between the United States and the Soviet Union that killed millions and destroyed civilization. In his remarks, Carl said the movie had, if anything, understated the damage that would be done by nuclear war. Even a small nuclear war would send up immense clouds of smoke and dust that would kill even the people in countries not hit by the bombs. The dust clouds would cut off sunlight and cause vast numbers of plants and animals to freeze to death. The dark and the cold would last for months, and most of the survivors would starve to death. Even a successful first strike might not protect the "winning" nation from the consequences of nuclear winter.

Carl made his comments in the early years of the Reagan Administration. Ronald Reagan had been elected president in 1980 with a promise to rebuild the U.S. military, with a special interest in upgrading the nation's nuclear arsenal. One of his first actions was to persuade the Western European leaders to allow the U.S. to place medium range nuclear missiles in their countries. Reagan was convinced that the Soviet Union would back down if the United States showed that it had no interest in reaching an accord with what he called the "Evil Empire."

Carl was deeply opposed to Reagan and his foreign policy objectives. He thought that Reagan was pushing the world to the brink of nuclear destruction. When Reagan suggested the U. S. should begin work on a "space shield" that would deflect nuclear missiles, Carl thought such a device would never work and would force the Soviets to attack first. Ultimately, it would only lure the U. S. into a false and dangerous sense of security. Carl thought defensive weapons in space were a waste of time and money.

Carl was so concerned over the dangers of Reagan's Strategic Defense Initiative (SDI) that not even a life-threatening illness could stop him from protesting. In 1983, he was hospitalized twice. Once for appendicitis, and again for a flare-up of his esophagus trouble. From his bed, he wrote a petition with Ann's help for Congress to vote against SDI. The petition was signed by an array of leaders and scientists from around the world.

It was the nuclear winter debate, however, that pushed Carl to the forefront of those opposed to the buildup of nuclear weapons proposed by the Reagan Administration. In October 1983, Carl participated in a two-day conference held in Washington D.C. It was called "The World after Nuclear War." In his speech to the assembled scientists, Carl described how a nuclear war would alter Earth's atmosphere. He said that the atmosphere would be so full of debris that most of the sunlight would be blocked out. Ground temperature would drop to levels that would make the planet uninhabitable. Carl argued that the only way to remove the threat of nuclear winter was for the United States and the Soviet Union to disassemble their nuclear weapons.

Although the *Cosmos* series had made him a household name—and Carl had always been controversial within the scientific community for his views on space exploration, global warming, and ozone depletion—his entrance into the nuclear winter debate made Carl one of the most highly controversial figures of the 1980s. He was instantly attacked by conservative politicians and commentators, as well as fellow scientists who either thought the nuclear winter theory was unsound or had their own more personal differences with Carl.

William F. Buckley, Jr., a long-time political journalist and talk show host, said that the theory was a fraud and that Carl and the others who popularized it knew that it was a fraud. Buckley claimed that Carl had sacrificed his scientific integrity to gain a political advantage. Other conservative writers claimed worse, some even suggested that Carl was a secret communist who was doing the work of the Soviets by undermining American resolve to stand up to what they saw as the world's greatest evil. It was true that Carl gained the attention of Mikhail

President Ronald Reagan proposed developing a "space shield" to protect the United States against nuclear attack.

Gorbachev and other leaders of the Soviet Union. Gorbachev also acted on Carl's suggestion that the two countries work together on a joint mission to Mars. No one knows how much impact the nuclear winter theory had on the decision, but on April 18, 1986, Mikhail Gorbachev announced the end of all nuclear testing in his country.

Carl's work against nuclear proliferation also won him an audience with Pope John Paul II. Although he was a confirmed agnostic—Carl held the view that nothing could be known about the existence of God—he decided to accept the invitation to visit the Pope. (He did refuse invitations to have dinner at the White House with President Reagan.) He and Ann traveled to Vatican City in Rome and discussed the nuclear winter theory with the leader of the Catholic Church.

In 1986, computer models began to suggest that the earth's cooling produced by nuclear war would be less severe than earlier suggested. By 1988, the evidence was inconclusive, but there was one result from the debate that was indisputable. Carl Sagan was a highly controversial figure in both scientific and political circles. He had angered the conservative administration and the academics on college campuses and in think tanks. He had become a polarizing figure in cultural, social, and political debates of the 1980s.

In 1985, the 8-million-channel Project META (Megachannel Extraterrestrial Assay) was turned on after Carl and Ann persuaded *Close Encounters* and *E.T.* director Steven Spielberg to donate $100,000 to the Planetary Society.

META had found several dozen intriguing signals, but none had ever repeated. Routine technical explanations—malfunctions of the instruments or interference from some terrestrial object, such as an airplane—were possible culprits. Carl calculated only one chance in 200 that the signals were some kind of accident. But, operating by his rule that "extraordinary claims require extraordinary evidence" he concluded that he still could not be sure. As he told a reporter, "It's certainly suggestive. You know, it sends a kind of chill down your spine."

Carl had several possible explanations for why alien signals have proven so elusive. It takes a huge amount of energy to send signals in all directions across such vast distances. Or, perhaps the aliens did not want to communicate with primitive creatures like us and were intentionally bypassing the obvious frequencies in the electromagnetic spectrum, choosing instead a medium that we have yet to discover. Or maybe, all the civilizations that develop radio astronomy technology soon destroy themselves.

Ann organized nuclear weapons and weapons testing

protests and asked Carl to attend. In September 1986, they were arrested along with 600 health care professionals at a nuclear test site in Nevada for committing "criminal trespass." They felt it was necessary to commit "civil disobedience"—violating the law to draw attention to a problem and then submitting peacefully to arrest—because the issue was too big to ignore. While Carl was giving a speech during the protest, a nuclear test weapon was detonated underground. When the U.S. announced another nuclear test date the following spring, they planned a bigger protest and invited celebrities such as Kris Kristofferson and Martin Sheen.

Even with all these controversies swirling around him, Carl was still letting his imagination play. In 1985, he wrote to Kip Thorne, a physicist at the University of California at Berkeley, for help with *Contact,* the science-fiction novel he and Ann were writing.

The novel, about Earth's first encounter with extraterrestrial intelligence, had begun as a movie script idea that Carl and Ann had developed just after they had finished *Cosmos.* The movie was intended to be yet another way for them to present their shared concerns—the possibility of extraterrestrial life, the importance of science, the public's fascination with UFOs, and the existence of God—to a wide audience.

The heroine, Dr. Ellie Arroway, is a radio astronomer

loosely based on a real person, Hypatia, an astronomer and mathematician who lived in ancient Egypt. In the story, Ellie hears a signal from her radio-telescope that makes sense—the aliens have sent back to us one of our own TV broadcasts, a documentary about Hitler, sent out decades before. She realizes that the star Vega, twenty-six light-years from Earth, is sending her a coded message which contains plans for the construction of a mysterious space vehicle that could transport a human to Vega. Ellie wants to be the one to go but faces prejudice because she is an atheist.

Finally allowed to go, Ellie travels instantaneously through the Galaxy and meets the alien, who is disguised as a human being. She then has trouble convincing people what she saw once she returns to Earth.

Carl had been hoping that Thorne could tell him how to use the idea of "black holes" to allow Ellie to travel almost instantly around the Galaxy.

What Thorne came up with was another idea then gaining prominence in astrophysics: "wormholes," or supposed tunnels through the space-time continuum. Space and time are like the curved surface of an apple. Wormholes allow you, the "worm," to go straight through the "apple." No one knows if wormholes actually exist, but Albert Einstein had developed equations that predicted them.

Carl liked the idea of wormholes, and his book was published later that year, in the fall of 1985. Some critics were not entirely thrilled by his first attempt at fiction, judging the writing and the characterization to be amateur. But, they praised the way it raised important ideas. The novel caught the attention of Hollywood producers and the rights to turn it into a movie were quickly bought. Carl was excited at the idea of a movie being made from his book. Through the experience of making *Cosmos*, he knew that it could be years before the movie premiered. He was willing to wait. His goal was for *Contact* to be turned into a realistic movie about the possibility of first contact with other life. He did not want it to be turned into "space opera."

Carl and Ann's nonfiction book *Comet* was released the same year as *Contact*. Both books topped the best-seller lists. Carl was now the most popular science writer in history.

In 1986, after a seven year trip, the *Voyager 2* probe, for which Carl had produced the records, began sending back remarkable photographs and data from Jupiter. Even though it had been expected to stop operating just past Saturn, the hardy probe sent back even more photographs and data from Saturn and its rings, and from the planet Uranus.

The *Voyager*'s success came in the middle of a con-

Contact's heroine, Ellie Arroway, monitors a radio telescope for alien feedback from Arecibo Observatory in Puerto Rico.

troversy between the "Moon-firsters" and the "Mars-firsters." The Moon-firsters argued for a slower approach to the exploration of space. Americans needed the experience of operating a permanent base on the Moon before attempting a dangerous trip to Mars.

Carl and 100,000 Mars-firsters signed a "Mars declaration" encouraging the human exploration of Mars as the first step toward placing human colonies on other planets and moons. The Mars-firsters opposed a return to the Moon as a pointless and expensive project that would only postpone a much more exciting Mars mission for many decades.

Carl had reversed his earlier opposition to manned space flight and now favored a Mars mission conducted jointly with the Soviet Union. He said, "I think people are bored with the moon. The moon rocks looked like the rocks in my back yard." Mars was "obviously the next great step for the human race." It was, he said, "a dynamic world, with vast volcanoes, its own two moons, ancient river valleys and climatic changes that may be relevant to climatic changes on Earth. It has an area equal to the land area on Earth, and the possibility of past or even present life."

In a way, these arguments were locked in a vacuum, even though Soviet President Mikhail Gorbachev had endorsed a U. S.-Soviet partnership and some members of Congress supported it. The U. S. government was no longer building the giant *Saturn 5* rocket that took *Apollo* astronauts to the Moon ten times. Mars was even less likely, since space scientists had yet to figure out how to keep people alive for the two-and-a-half-year trip there and back. The cost alone might make such a trip unlikely. A ship that could fly to Mars would be too heavy to be lifted off Earth in one piece, so it would have to be assembled in sections in low Earth orbit—a process that would take about a year to complete and cost tens of billions of dollars.

One reason for Carl's abiding interest in Mars was his support of the theory that an asteroid had smashed into Earth 65 million years ago, killing off the dinosaurs. If we could better date the craters and periods of volcanic activity on Mars, astronomers could figure out how important comet impacts were in causing Martian volcanoes. That would tell us how the planet had cooled and when there were volcanic releases of water vapor and other gases. And that, in turn, would help us to better understand the relationship between comet, asteroid, or meteor impacts and volcanic activity on Earth.

As much as he wanted to see an expedition to Mars, Carl the dreamer was also Carl the practical thinker. He wanted to encourage cooperation with the Soviets as a way of encouraging the development of peaceful relations between the superpowers. By 1989, he was proposing joint research aboard the Russian space station, *Mir.* Teams of Russian and American astronauts would measure the effects of radiation in space and solar flares and experiment with artificial gravity and in-space construction.

Though the end of the 1980s was a bad time for achieving international cooperation on a manned expedition to Mars, something else was happening that tested one of Carl's longest-standing research interests: The possibility of life on other planets was being questioned anew.

Carl and other astronomers had long wondered whether any of the organic material that formed the chemical building blocks of life could have come to Earth in an intense bombardment of comets and asteroids billions of years ago. As a young scientist, he had dismissed the idea, but new theories and new data compelled him to take a second look. For instance, a computer model revealed that tar-like mixtures of organic molecules in asteroids and comets could have survived the searing heat encountered on entry into the thick atmosphere of ancient Earth and been ejected into the oceans.

Carl had reason to think about such alien sources of organic material and the life they might give rise to in the most unlikely places, because he was a member of the

Voyager 2 imaging team. He was now beginning to see the pictures that the spaceship was beaming back from Neptune as it continued on its journey out of the solar system. The photographs revealed a planet with turbulent weather surrounded by faint rings. Its moon, Triton, which looked like a lumpy snowball, was coated in parts with organic material that might be similar to the material from which life had sprung on Earth.

This was not the first time that the *Voyager 2* and its twin, *Voyager 1*, had given rise among the scientists overseeing their flight to talk of life on the outer planets. One of Jupiter's moons, Europa, was found to have an ocean beneath a thick shell of ice. If Europa were seeded with microorganisms, it just might sustain life.

Now, as *Voyager 2* approached Triton, the moon began to reveal signs of methane gas—a basic element in the formation of life. As Carl had himself demonstrated in a laboratory, simple compounds had been bombarded on Earth billions of years ago by lightning to produce more complex organic material until reaching a critical point, and life was created.

The *Voyager* scientists were curious to see if such a process was occurring on Triton, even though the surface temperature of minus 350 degrees made it extremely unlikely that the critical point could have been reached.

Ever the dreamer, Carl visualized Triton as a world

with a liquid-nitrogen ocean rich in primordial organic sludge. He even named the red sludge "tholin," from the Greek word for "muddy." "All the chemicals are elaborate poisons," he added, making Triton even more intriguing. But when *Voyager 2* actually got close enough to Triton for high-resolution photographs, the results were disappointing. Instead of oceans, there was ice colored pink by radiation, snowdrifts, and glaciers. Carl's vast fields of "tholin" were curious red and blue regions whose content was hard to determine.

Even so, the moment of approach was highly dramatic, and to celebrate, the Planetary Society hosted a party for the *Voyager* team. Ann had arranged a special surprise for Carl and the party goers. After Carl spoke, the lights went out, the strum of an electric guitar was heard, and out walked legendary rock-n-roller Chuck Berry singing "Johnny B. Goode"—the same recording that had been sent into space with the *Voyager* over a decade earlier. People began dancing, and Berry cried out, "How 'bout that li'l ole Voyager way out past Neptune?"

After a successful twelve-year voyage through our solar system, *Voyager* headed out into the vastness between the stars.

Chapter Seven

Disputes

By now it seemed as if there were no controversy Carl would not weigh in on, or in which his considerable influence and popularity would not prove advantageous for his allies.

In 1990, he headed a group of thirty-two internationally eminent scientists delivering an open letter to the North American religious community. The letter stated that there was no technological fix for unparalleled worldwide environmental devastation. They called upon religious leaders and churches to react to the crisis as the only social agents with the ethical power to respond to "crimes against creation."

"Molecules," Carl said, "don't observe national boundaries." He was talking about the pollutants that caused ozone-layer depletion and the greenhouse effect. The deterioration of the protective ozone layer in the Earth's atmosphere had been linked mainly to release of refrigerant chemicals called chloro-fluoro-carbons (CFCs). Carbon dioxide from the burning of oil, coal, and other fossil fuels had created a greenhouse effect which led to global warming. The threat of such pollutants rising into the air from one country and causing problems for the whole world became an organizing image for Carl's effort.

Toward the end of the Gulf War against Iraq in January 1991, Carl finally got the chance to test his "nuclear winter" theory. The results were not what he expected. The Iraqi army had set fires in the oil fields of neighboring Kuwait. Carl and his colleagues feared that smoke from the fires might cause drastic changes in the weather. On January 22, when the first oil wells were set on fire, Carl appeared on the television program *Nightline* and painted a terrifying picture of the world-wide devastation he thought would follow the oil field fires.

"We think the net effects will be very similar to the explosion of the Indonesian volcano Tambora in 1815, which resulted in the year 1816 being known as the year without a summer," he said. "There were massive agricultural failures in North America and in Western Europe, and very serious human suffering, and in some cases starvation. Especially for South Asia, that seems to be in the cards, and perhaps for a significant fraction of the Northern Hemisphere as well."

From the start of the Gulf War, however, it had been clear that the amount of smoke from the Kuwaiti oil fires would be far less than that of a full-scale nuclear war—less than one percent as much. The dispute pointed out the difficulty of making massive predictions about the weather and the atmosphere.

Events outside of our atmosphere raised more questions about nuclear winter. In July 1994, the comet Shoemaker-Levy 9 crashed into Jupiter. Based on estimates from the Hubble Space Telescope, which provided a close-up look at the crash, scientists estimated that if a similar comet crashed into Earth, it would release energy equal to 100 million megatons of TNT, or 10,000 times the total destructive force of the entire world's nuclear arsenal at the peak of the Cold War.

Carl noted that the comet was about the same size as the one believed to have hit Earth 65 million years ago, killing some seventy-five percent of all species, including the dinosaurs. It left traces of the element iridium, a telltale sign of cometary debris. Significant quantities of carbon in the sedimentary layer suggest a massive fire raged across landmasses. Below this sedimentary layer, extensive fossil evidence shows that the world had been teeming with dinosaurs. Above this layer, they were gone.

As Carl reconstructed the probable results according

to the nuclear winter scenario, debris from the impact in the upper atmosphere had cut off sunlight long enough to kill plant life. With the air temperature much cooler, those plants still alive had faced prolonged frigid weather and terrible winters. The ozone layer had been depleted and global acid rain ravaged vegetation everywhere.

How much risk did he think we faced from comets? "The Earth moves in a swarm of debris, comets, and asteroids, little worlds that orbit the Sun, but usually not in such regular circular orbits," Carl explained. There are probably 2,000 near-Earth asteroids bigger than one kilometer across, and an estimated 200,000 larger than 100 meters across. The probability of Earth being hit by a ten-kilometer comet was extremely low, an impact occurring on the average once every 100 million years. The frequency of impact by one-kilometer comets was closer to one in 100,000 years.

Suppose we discovered a comet on target for Earth? What if we had only sixteen months warning, as with Shoemaker-Levy 9? What could be done? Carl thought it would be wise to locate and count all the large comets and Earth-crossing asteroids. An asteroid about two miles in diameter came within two million miles of Earth in December 1992. It is scheduled to come within a million miles of Earth in the year 2004.

Perhaps there was a use for nuclear weapons, after all.

Carl suggested loading rockets with nuclear weapons to deflect comets and asteroids. Others supported the use of nuclear weapons to deter collisions in only the most extreme cases. The efficacy of nuclear weapons to destroy comets and asteroids before they collided with Earth was questionable. No one really understood the physical properties of asteroids. In addition, there are inherent risks in the very existence of such weapons, and by international agreement it is illegal to detonate them in space. Carl feared that a nuclear defense system capable of deflecting an approaching object would be used by a terrorist organization to knock a harmless object into a collision course with Earth. It was an especially complicated question.

That same year, Daniel Goldin, the newly installed NASA Administrator, consulted with Carl on NASA's future plans during dozens of meetings. Carl argued against NASA's habit of launching rare, costly probes. In 1992, the agency was scheduled to launch only one spacecraft to Mars, the orbiter *Observer,* that would cost $1 billion. It would be the nation's first mission to Mars in seventeen years.

Carl persuaded Goldin that such costly flights were wasteful. Within a year, NASA had adopted a new approach. Low-cost orbiters and landers would be sent every two years as Mars and Earth came into alignment.

If one failed, there would still be others—an advantage that became apparent when NASA lost communication with the *Observer* in August 1993 as it neared Mars. The low-cost approach paid off when the Mars *Pathfinder* landed in 1996 and created massive public interest with its miniature rover.

Carl also urged Goldin and the NASA leadership to increase the agency's skills in looking for signs of alien life. In response, NASA set up an Astrobiology Institute, bringing together experts in the field of exobiology.

In 1992, Stanley Miller, the chemist who had pioneered the study of the origin of life with Harold Urey, nominated Carl for election into the National Academy of Sciences. He was challenged, and a debate ensued at the academy. Miller argued that Carl's scientific work, such as his research on the atmosphere of Venus, was being overlooked in favor of criticizing his career in televison and popular literature. The anti-Carl faction countered that if Carl's popular work were closely examined, the "hard science" beneath it would be found deficient. One member reasoned, "If he had not done television, he probably would be in the academy." His admission was eventually denied.

Philip Morrison, a distinguished physicist at MIT, thought Carl's omission "was just plain envy." Kip Thorne called his rejection a "shameful decision" to blackball the

NASA is able to obtain information about our solar system with high-tech devices such as the Hubble Space Telescope.

country's most recognizable scientist. As a consolation prize, the NAS awarded Carl the Public Welfare Medal.

Carl decided not to dwell on the insult. He claimed he had assumed years earlier that he would never get in. "To discover that it was still a live issue surprised me more than learning that there were people opposed to my membership." Ann responded: "It was painful. It seemed like a kind of unsolicited slight. We hadn't done anything, he hadn't done anything. It was clear from people who were present at the time that there was something venomous about it."

Carl conceded that his phenomenal range of interests and subjects could be seen as a weakness. "It's a question of the balance between breadth and depth. Everyone has limitations of time and ability. Certainly it's true that if you spend a lot of time on breadth, you must be losing something on depth....But I also see scientists who are bummed out after a while, and their productivity declines in their narrowly circumscribed field."

Back home in Ithaca, Cornell students were "honoring" Carl in their own way when The *Cornell Review* offered an "I Touched Carl Sagan Contest" to the university's undergraduates.

Chapter Eight

The Stuff of Life

On his sixtieth birthday in November 1994, 300 friends, colleagues, journalists, scientists, and artists spent an evening praising Carl at Cornell. Attending were Ann, his first wife, Lynn Alexander Margulis, and his five children (including the youngest, Samuel Democritus Druyan Sagan, born in 1991). Everyone reached for superlatives to describe Carl.

An undergraduate announced that he had majored in science after a single encounter with Carl. A graduate student in astronomy had changed the subject of his doctoral dissertation to planetary atmospheres after hearing Carl describe his work. The chair of Carl's department read a letter from a student in Africa who had begun an astronomy club in his village after reading the book version of *Cosmos.* The crowd was stunned when the student, who had been flown to Ithaca for the occasion, came forward to meet Carl. One young Cornell undergraduate offered a poetic tribute describing how Carl had opened her eyes to the stars—those "pinpricks of infinity" as she put it. Both Cornell's astronomy department and a friend of Carl's from Greece presented him with identical offerings: busts of Venus, the Goddess of Love—the planetary subject of Carl's doctoral dissertation at the University of Chicago more than three decades earlier. Letters were read from top officials of international governments, and an astronomer announced that two small asteroids she had discovered circling the Sun between the orbits of Mars and Jupiter were now named "2709 Sagan" and "4973 Druyan." The asteroids are in perpetual orbit around the Sun like two wedding bands.

Russian space scientist Roald Sagdeev (who had married President Eisenhower's granddaughter, Susan) told how the Kremlin had been influenced by Carl. When President Ronald Reagan came to Moscow, President Mikhail Gorbachev urged him to endorse a joint Soviet-American manned expedition to Mars. Reagan welcomed the idea, Sagdeev said, until he was told Carl supported it, too. Carl's opposition to Reagan's Strategic Defense Initiative caused the president to drop out of the Soviet project.

Carl responded to all the praise by speaking passionately about the dangers of human self-centeredness, a theme he illustrated by pointing to a tiny blue dot pro-

Cornell University honored Carl on his sixtieth birthday by throwing him a grand party.

(© Cornell University Photography.)

jected on a huge screen above him. It was a photograph of Earth taken by *Voyager* as it left the solar system. He spoke eloquently: "Our planet is a lonely speck in the great enveloping cosmic dark....There is perhaps no better demonstration of the folly of human conceits than this distant image of our tiny world. To me, it underscores our responsibility to deal more kindly with one another, and to preserve and cherish the pale blue dot, the only home we've ever known."

During the two days of celebrations, the director of the Jet Propulsion Lab, which controls NASA probes in deep space, speculated about the possibility of life on Saturn's giant moon, Titan. Carl's old colleague and fellow SETI member Frank Drake brought the audience up to date on the search.

In early 1995, Ann discovered a bruise on Carl's arm that was slow to heal. While Carl and Ann were negotiating the arrangements for the film *Contact*, Carl had a blood test. The doctor's report was somber. Carl had *myelodysplasia*, a rare bone marrow disease that could lead to leukemia. Without a bone marrow transplant, he could be dead in six months. On March 13, 1995, Carl announced that he would take a medical leave of absence from Cornell.

Carl called his sister, Carol, who was the best donor candidate. Before he could finish asking, Carol graciously told him, "You got it. Whatever it is—liver, lung—it's yours." They went through the painful transplant procedure in April 1995 at Seattle's Fred Hutchinson Cancer Research Center. To prevent his body from rejecting the marrow, he had to wipe out his immune system. In one sitting he swallowed seventy-two pills labeled "BIOHAZARD." These pills alone would have killed him had he not had the bone marrow transplant immediately.

While Carl spent the next five weeks recovering in the Seattle hospital, an unexplained fire swept through the Laboratory for Planetary Studies at Cornell. Many experiments and documents were destroyed, but no one was hurt. Officials wondered if dangerous chemicals had caused the fire, or had been emitted in the smoke. The building was temporarily shut down.

As Carl attempted to regain his strength, he resumed work. After years of delay, the film version of his novel, *Contact,* had been put into production. Carl and Ann worked with the producer on every aspect of the film. Carl was determined to make an intelligent movie about alien contact. He had voiced serious concerns about the way earlier Hollywood movies had dealt with the subject. The aliens were featured as either evil destructive monsters or as sweet and innocent victims of human cruelty. Carl and Ann also wanted *Contact* to capture how scientists work.

They asked other working scientists for their input.

Although his health was poor, Carl worked hard in the pre-production stages of the film. He helped to pick the actors and was delighted when Jodie Foster signed on to play the lead character, Ellie Arroway. He made many suggestions about how the film should be shot.

Carl took great pleasure in working on the movie. He even thought for a while that his strength was returning. But, just as things were looking brighter, he learned in December that the transplant had been unsuccessful. He returned to Seattle for chemotherapy and another bone marrow transplant from Carol. It seemed that he and Ann would have to stay in Seattle for many months. The recurrence of Carl's illness alarmed his doctors. His body was already weakened from his earlier transplant. They feared he would not survive further treatment.

Ann moved to Seattle and enrolled Samuel and Sasha in school. Carl was in the hospital for months after the second transplant. Slowly, the gloom lightened. The treatment was apparently a success. He told a reporter, "No *myelodysplasia*. No anomalous cells. Nothing." As soon as he was able, Carl got back to work. His doctors hoped for the best.

To demonstrate that his taste for vigorous controversy was still intact, Carl held forth at a conference that the media's "glorification of stupidity...reassur[es] people it's all right not to know anything—that in a way it's cool." His vigor at the podium affected Ann, who listened from a table and alternately beamed and wiped away tears as he spoke. She called his battle with disease during the past five months in Seattle "a horrible, wonderful time....His character and courage is as formidable as his intelligence."

Carl was determined to keep working. A prediction made two decades earlier in *The Cosmic Connection* that planets were common throughout the galaxy was rapidly being confirmed by the Hubble Space Telescope. Carl was interviewed by the PBS program *Nova* on its show about so-called "alien abduction." Carl responded to thousands of claims by ordinary people that they had been kidnapped by creatures from outer space and subjected to scary experiments. Such claims had been made ever since 1947, when reports of sightings of UFOs had started to be made public. Government investigators had dismissed most as hoaxes, aircraft, or celestial bodies. But, many Americans continued to believe that aliens from other worlds were visiting Earth. It was those reports that had inspired Steven Spielberg's *Close Encounters of the Third Kind*.

What concerned Carl about the UFO abduction stories was not only the complete lack of any credible evidence—a piece of metal or strange instrument from a spaceship—but also the possibility that dreams, lies, published news stories about other "abductees," and hypnosis by well-meaning abduction investigators, had all played a role in the claims. The abduction stories were faulty for another reason. Why were the aliens breeding human beings one by one? Why not steal some DNA and breed whole colonies of people to experiment on?

He dealt with many of these questions in *The Demon-Haunted World*, one of two books he published in 1996. It was a collection of essays not only on alien abductions but on other examples of controversial issues, such as "recovered" memories of Satanic ritual child abuse, faster-than-light travel, and perpetual motion machines.

Carl's health had not improved as much as he had hoped it would, and he continued to struggle with illness. While there was still no sign of abnormal cells, he was clearly not well. He was underweight and fatigued easily.

In early December, Carl visited with NASA Administrator Daniel Goldin for the last time. Carl's blue jeans hung from his gaunt frame. For hours in Goldin's office and then over dinner in a nearby restaurant, he presented his vision of the future of space exploration. Goldin marveled at his intensity. "A man on his deathbed. This is the Carl Sagan I love, a man so full of hope and optimism that he never gave up. He never gave up."

Even with Carl's personal relationship with the administrator, he had been unable to keep NASA from canceling its SETI program that year. The search for extraterrestrial signals had become entirely dependent on private fund-raising, much of it by the 100,000 members of the Planetary Society, which operates radio-telescopes in Massachusetts and Argentina.

The end of government financing for SETI was irritating to everyone involved in the search, because the odds were so strong that there was life out there. "Organic matter, the stuff of life, is absolutely everywhere," Carl said. "Comets are made one-quarter of organic matter. Many worlds in the outer solar system are coated with dark organic matter. On Titan, organic matter is falling from the skies like manna from Heaven. The cold diffuse interstellar gas is loaded with organic matter. There doesn't seem to be an impediment about the stuff of life." And, this organic matter has plenty of places to land and start turning into living, evolving organisms.

In July 1996, Carl and Ann returned to Seattle to face a third bone marrow transplant. First, Carl was given a full-body radiation treatment, then he and Carol went through the grueling procedure all over again. On the day he left the hospital, bald and gaunt from the chemotherapy, he was interviewed on network TV about the discovery of an asteroid in Antarctica that showed fossil traces, possibly left by Martian microbes. Although he was dubious about the microbe hypothesis, he gave a poetic description about the possibility of life on other worlds and rallied behind continued exploration: "We need a multi-planet exploration," he said, "in order to settle the question of life on other planets."

Carl and Ann and their family celebrated Thanksgiving 1996 in Ithaca. On December 4, Carl appeared on an episode of *Nightline*. Shortly afterwards, his weakened body contracted pneumonia. Carl Sagan died on December 20, 1996. He was sixty-two years old.

Ann would later describe their last two years together as being on a "roller coaster of hopes dashed, raised, and dashed again." In the coming months, Cornell hosted two memorial services for Carl, his Laboratory for Planetary Studies was permanently closed, and the movie *Contact* was released in July 1997.

Carl is remembered as a passionate scientist who brought his favorite subject forward for public appreciation. "Ask courageous questions," he urged. "Do not be satisfied with superficial answers. Be open to wonder and at the same time subject all claims to knowledge, without exception, to intense skeptical scrutiny. Be aware of human fallibility. Cherish your species and your planet."

Major Works

Carl contributed chapters to many books, wrote radio and television scripts, many with Ann Druyan, and wrote articles for encyclopedias. He contributed more than 600 articles to scientific journals, and dozens of articles to popular periodicals. He was also the editor of many scientific journals. His curriculum vitae runs about 250 pages.

1961—The Atmospheres of Mars and Venus (with W.W. Kellogg)

1966—Intelligent Life in the Universe (with I. S. Shklovskii)

1970—Planetary Exploration: The Condon Lectures

1971—Planetary Atmospheres (ed. with T. Owen and H. J. Smith)

The Air War in Indochina (with R. Littauer and others)

1972—UFO's: A Scientific Debate (ed. with T. Page)

1973—The Cosmic Connection: An Extraterrestrial Perspective

Communication With Extraterrestrial Intelligence (CETI), editor

Mars and the Mind of Man (with R. Bradbury, A. C. Clarke, B. Murray, and W. Sullivan)

Life Beyond Earth and the Mind of Man (with R. Berendzen, A. Montagu, P. Morrison, K. Stendhal and G. Wald)

1977—The Dragons of Eden: Speculations on the Evolution of Human Intelligence

1978 —The Search for Extraterrestrial Intelligence (with P. Morrison and others)

Murmurs of Earth: The Voyager Interstellar Record (with F. Drake, A. Druyan, J. Lomberg, L. Sagan and T. Ferris)

The Martian Landscape (with T. A. Mutch and other members of the Viking Lander Imaging Team)

1979—Broca's Brain: Reflections on the Romance of Science

Machine Intelligence and Robotics: Report of the NASA Study Group (Chairman of Study Group; many co-authors)

1980—Cosmos

1984—The Fallacy of Star Wars: Why Space Weapons Can't Protect Us (with R. Garwin et. al.)

Atomkrieg und Climakatastroph (Atomic War and Climatic Catastrophe)

The Cold And The Dark: The World After Nuclear War (with P. R. Ehrlich, D. Kennedy and W. O. Roberts)

1985—Contact: A Novel
Comet (with A. Druyan)

1989—A Path Where No Man Thought: Nuclear Winter and the End of the Arms Race (with R. Turco)

1992—Shadows of Forgotten Ancestors: A Search for Who We Are (with A. Druyan)

1994—Pale Blue Dot: A Vision of the Human Future in Space

1996—The Demon-Haunted World: Science as a Candle in the Dark

1997—Billions and Billions

Timeline

1934—Born in Brooklyn, New York, on November 9.
1939—Attends New York World's Fair.
1947-51—Attends Rahway High School, Rahway, New Jersey.
1951-55—Undergraduate at the University of Chicago.
1956—Earns master's degree in physics from University of Chicago. Publishes first paper, "Radiation and the Origin of the Gene."
1957—Marries Lynn Alexander on June 16.
1958—Dorian Soloman Sagan born.
1960—Earns PhD. in astronomy and astrophysics from University of Chicago. Jeremy Ethan Sagan born.
1962—Hired by Harvard University. Attends Green Bank meeting.
1963—Divorces Lynn Alexander.
1966—Collaborates with I. S. Shklovskii on *Intelligent Life in the Universe*.
1968—Leaves Harvard. Marries Linda Salzman on April 6. Hired at Cornell University.
1969—Member of the *Apollo 11* briefing team.
1970—Granted tenure at Cornell. Nicholas Julian Zapata Sagan born.

1972—Appears on the *Tonight Show*. Designs *Pioneer* plaque. Publishes *The Cosmic Connection: An Extraterrestrial Perspective*.

1976—Designs *Voyager* record.

1977—Wins the Pulitzer Prize for *The Dragons of Eden*.

1977-80—Creates *Cosmos*. Founds the Planetary Society.

1981—Divorce with Linda Salzman is finalized. Marries Ann Druyan on June 1.

1982—Alexandra Rachel Druyan Sagan born.

1985—Publishes the novel *Contact*.

1986—Arrested for "criminal trespass" at a U.S. nuclear weapons test site in Nevada.

1991—Samuel Democritus Sagan born.

1992—Nominated for election to the National Academy of Sciences.

1994—Celebrates sixtieth birthday at Cornell.

1995—Diagnosed with *myelodysplasia*.

1996—Publishes *The Demon-Haunted World*. Dies on December 20.

Bibliography

Achenbach, Joel. "The Final Frontier? All Carl Sagan Wants to Do Is Understand the Universe. All He Needs Is Time," *Washington Post,* May 30, 1996.

——"A Bright Star in The Cosmos," *Washington Post,* December 21, 1996.

Arana-Ward, Marie. "Carl Sagan," *Washington Post,* January 9, 1994.

Barnes, Bart. "Carl Sagan, Who Reached for the Stars and Touched Millions, Dies at 62," *Washington Post,* December 21, 1996.

Beaudan, Eric. "Peaceful Lessons From Space," *Kiwanis Magazine*, January, 1989.

Broad, William J. "Even in Death, Carl Sagan's Influence Is Still Cosmic," *The New York Times Magazine,* December 1, 1998.

Burbank, James. "Can Eco-Justice Go Mainstream?" *National Catholic Reporter*, June 6, 1997.

"Carl Sagan: A Cosmic Celebrity." New York: A&E Television Networks (home video).

"Carl Sagan: A Tribute," *Odyssey*, April, 1998.

Cohen, Daniel. *Carl Sagan: Superstar Scientist*, New York: Dodd, Mead & Company, 1987.

"Comets May Have Supplied Earth With Chemicals Of Life," *Earth Science*, Summer, 1989.

Contemporary Authors: New Revision Series, Volume 36, Detroit: Gale Research Inc, 1992.

Current Biography. New York: The H.W. Wilson Company, 1970.

Dawson, Bill. "Urgent Action Urged On The Environment," *Houston Chronicle*, May 6, 1990.

Desonie, Dana. "The Threat From Space," *Earth*, Aug. 1996.

Drell, Adrienne. "Sagan in Chicago: Billions of Memories," *Chicago Sun-Times*, December 22, 1996.

Druyan, Ann. "Billions and Billions," *Breakthroughs.*

Friedman, Louis D. "Steps To Mars II: A Conference Report," *Planetary Report,* November/December 1995.

Golden, Frederic. "A Celestial Event for a Premier Stargazer," *Los Angeles Times*, October 19, 1994.

Grossman, Ron. "Aristotle of Academe," *Chicago Tribune*, November 17, 1989.

Hall, Stephen S. "Time Travel," *California Magazine*, Issue 1, 1990.

Harris, Art. "Second View: Sagan on 'Encounters'; Astronomer Calls Portraying Beings From Outer Space As Humanoids 'Earth Chauvinism'," *Washington Post,* December 16, 1977.

Hirschman, Ron. *SETI: The Radio Search* http://setiathome.ssl.berkeley.edu

"Kidnapped by UFOs?," *Nova* (PBS), April 1, 1997.

Lewontin, Richard. "Billions and Billions of Demons," *The New York Review Of Books,* January 9, 1997.

Longley, Richard. "Destination Mars," *Rotunda,* Winter, 1988/89.

McDonough, Thomas R. "A Quantum Leap For SETI: Project Beta Goes On—Line," *Planetary Report,* March/April 1996.

Meyer, Tom. "Heads Up! When Worlds Collide," *Final Frontier*, January/February 1994.

Oliver, Myrna. "Astronomer Sagan Dies; Helped Popularize Science...." *Los Angeles Times,* December 21, 1996.

Poundstone, William. Carl Sagan: *A Life in the Cosmos*, New York: Henry Holt, 1999.

Powell, Corey S. "A Pale Blue Planet Mourns the Passing of a Passionate Scientist," *Scientific American,* January, 1997.

Rampino, Michael. "Dinosaurs, Comets and Volcanoes," *New Scientist,* February 18, 1989.

Reinhart, Al. "Gerry's World," *Air & Space*, April/May 1989.

Rogers, Michael. "From Molecules And Quasars," *Washington Post,* May 27, 1979.

Sagan, Carl. *The Demon-Haunted World: Science as a Candle in the Dark*, New York: Random House, 1996.

——"In praise of the great teachers: three students recall lessons of a lifetime," *Washington Post,* Novem ber 6, 1994.

Sagan, Carl and Druyan, Ann. "Real Patriots Ask Questions," *Parade*, September 8, 1991.

Sawyer, Kathy. "The Search For A Signpost In Space," *Washington Post National Weekly Edition,* May 8-14, 1989.

Shapiro, Walter. "Carl Sagan's Last Mistake; A Road Map To Earth And Schematics Of Us," *The Washington Post Magazine,* December 28, 1980.

Shostak, Seth. "Extraterrestrial Searches: Listening for Life," *Astronomy*, October 1992.

Tourtellot, Jonathan. "Neptune Unveiled," *Earthwatch*, December 1989.

"Unbeliever's Quest," *Newsweek*, March 31, 1997.

Vrazo, Fawn. "The Future: Back To The Moon, Or Onward To Mars?," *St. Paul Pioneer Press Dispatch,* July 16, 1989.

Zimmer, Carl. "Environment: Ecowar," *Discover,* January 1992.

Index